AF433664

People's Mall and Amusement Park; Bhopal, India

**EASTERN
STRUCTURES**

editor

R. W. Watkins

creative consultants

Jim Wilson
Jacqueline Jones

printing / production

Nocturnal Iris
World Headquarters
in conjunction with KDP
and Amazon.com

Cover, page 2 and above:
Er. Vijay Shah (YouTube)

Eastern Structures is published
four times per year by
Nocturnal Iris Publications

PO Box 111
Moreton's Harbour, NL
A0G 3H0 Canada

Postal submissions of poems, essays,
reviews or related material should be
accompanied by an SASE (in
Canada) or an SAE + IRC (outside of
Canada). Electronic submissions
should be e-mailed to
nocturnaliris@gmail.com.

EASTERN STRUCTURES

Number 18 • Spring, 2021 • ISBN: 9798513006107

CONTENTS

4   forward
37   about the contributors

e s s a y

25   'Focus on Raymond Roseliep: His Haiku Journey' by
      Jim Wilson

t h e   p o e m s

Carew, Marla.....................................pp. 18, 21, 22, 23 and 36
Denehan, Steve.......................................pp. 20, 21, 22 and 36
Grandstaff, Sari...pp. 19, 20 and 21
Heflin, Rose Menyon.................................pp. 17, 18 and 23
Hurley, Foster...p. 24
Israel, David Raphael...pp. 9, 10, 11, 13, 14, 15, 16, 23 and 34
Jenckes, Norma...p. 23
Lignori, Priscilla.................…........pp. 18, 19, 20, 22, 23 and 36
Lignori, James...pp. 24 and 36
Liùsaidh...p. 6
Lustbader, Michael..p. 19
Rahim, Muhammad Sallahudin Bin Abdul.....................p. 35
Shields, David...p. 33
Stone, Alison...pp. 5 and 7
Torgersen, Eric...p. 8
Watkins, R. W.......................pp. 18, 20, 21, 22, 23, 24 and 36
Wilson, Jim...pp. 19 and 20
Wilson, Michael...p. 17 and 24
Woerner, Danielle...pp. 18, 19 and 36

This issue lovingly dedicated to the memory of
Rachel Claudine Watkins (1937–2021)

Forward

Contemplating the behaviour of certain 'factions' of North American poets again just recently, I experienced another minor epiphany.

It was while reading one of Jim Wilson's reiterative yet informative Facebook posts in the Formal Haiku group that I experienced said revelation. Wilson's post was outlining the dubious "hegemonic" actions of haiku organisations—e.g., the Haiku Society of America's campaign to encourage major dictionaries to adopt their "conjured" definition of haiku; the same society's attempts to manipulate early online search engines so that haiku sites not aligning with HSA tastes would be classified as 'faux haiku'; petitions to drop 5-7-5 submission guidelines—when I found myself asking, *Where have I heard all this before?*

The retrofitting and outright inventing of 'age-old' rules and tenets ... the controlling and rewriting of history ... the nullifying of other interpretations and approaches ... the demanding of official recognition or status in the first place – Aren't these the earmarks of the various pagan, Wiccan or 'witch' covens and the like over the past three decades?

Think about it. When most of us Gen-X'ers were growing up in the 1970s and '80s, such fringe groups existed only at the underground level. There was the occasional romanticised story in music magazines and celebrity biographies about hippies-turned-witches, Jimmy Page's occult bookstore and residence at Aleister Crowley's mansion, the Rolling Stones' and Jim Morrison's tumultuous affairs and witchy weddings with Anita Pallenberg and Patricia Kennealy (who once called me a "pretentious ass"), etc.; but nothing that caught the mainstream media's attention. Then sometime around 1990 the American daytime chat shows decided that such darkly erotic fare might be a fun cash-cow to milk—possibly even juicier than Klan moms and father-daughter incest. From that point onward the flood gates were open to a barrage of racy, new-agey, Mickey Mouse magik and malarkey—indeed a veritable witches' brew of Brocken, broomsticks, Beltane and bullshit that left many a Religious Studies professor laughing in hysterics. "The witches were out in full force on this Summer Solstice," reported a smiling anchorwoman on some Boston news show circa 1994, as some poor disillusioned slob in a white robe thumped downward on an Irish bodhran as if it were a Native American war drum. It wasn't long, of course, before a few gadflies started petitioning for official recognition under the law. Some continue to demand a paid holiday on the 31st of October—the Samhain of old Celtic lore.

The fact that most of such pagan practices actually find their origins in Margaret Murray's 1920s speculations about pagan 'holdovers' in Medieval Europe, and that Murray's wild and elaborate claims have been debunked for decades, is conveniently ignored. Also swept under the orgy rug are the arbitrary bog-slayings and other ritual sacrifices of those ancient Celtic priests, the druids—the original hippies, if we are to buy the talk-show tripe.

So, given their penchant for burying history and changing the rules to suit their situation, I guess I shouldn't be surprised that such a large portion of free-verse haiku poets in recent decades—including executive and/or influential organisation members—has identified as *pagan* or *Wiccan*, or at least dabbled in said contrived esoteric hoodoo. How many letters and emails have I received from such poets since the mid 1990s that have signed off with "Blessings" or "Blessed Be"!

Compare this to the religious or philosophical inclinations of *formal* haiku poets as exemplified by those typically found in a magazine like *Eastern Structures*. Is it merely a coincidence that the majority of *Eastern Structures* contributors identify either as Christian, Jewish or Muslim or as atheistic or agnostic?

In the forward to ES No. 11 I discussed the similarities between the haiku organisations and religious cults in regards to recruitment, indoctrination, conformity vs. ostracism, etc. When you factor in the dubious pagan element, the comparison looks even more ridiculously accurate—if not a little chilling.

It never occurred to me up until now that it may in fact have been the dark Celtic elements of my lengthy 'October Twilight' sequence that sold *Lynx* editors Jane and Werner Reichhold on my work in the first place back in 1995. Also, in all my years of contributing regularly to the said journal, I never once envisioned the Reichholds in a 'skyclad' moment. Now, having considered the full ramifications of such pagan practices, suddenly I can't unsee such a garish vision.

Look for ES No. 19 in late August or early September, and keep the faith—or lack thereof.

R. W. Watkins

Garbage Truck and Blue Jay

Alison Stone

In my day, children made to play outside.
Lemon juice in our hair, we lay outside.

Places color and name us. Tight wife-walk
in her home town. Loose-hipped sashay outside.

Heart calm, hair sticky with sea salt. Nose
and shoulders peeling from her day outside.

Merlin bats at the window, would trade nine
safe lives for the enticing prey outside.

Deal struck with her inner boss – Saturday
spent on cleaning and chores. Sunday outside.

Though the calendar page shows snow-coated
kids on a hill, it feels like May outside.

My mother's scarves donated, her warm coat.
We'll sleep with sorrow, she'll decay outside.

Depression's unrelenting monochrome
is in synch with the turbid gray outside.

So much unnoticed sweetness. Swallowed love.
The past a locked room. No way outside.

His morning meditation punctured by
garbage trucks and a shrieking jay outside.

Moon-tranced Endymion, motionless. One
silver shaft in his heart, one ray outside.

Keep your cathedrals, synagogues, and mosques.
I read scripture in leaf veins. Pray outside.

Poor screen-bleary Alison. Too much harsh
blue light. You need a holiday outside.

Previously published in *Zombies at the Disco* (Jacar Press), 2020

Problem Mum

Liùsaidh

People nowadays do not understand what cruelty is... Ordinary cruelty is simply stupidity...
Wherever you have centralisation, you have stupidity. — Oscar Wilde

Autism's a political condition. We know, we've cause to poll you, problem mum.
For it's not the *child's* challenging behaviour that takes the greatest toll. You problem mum!

It starts when you can't get a diagnosis. Your happy child regresses, disappears.
They run a class to teach the 'failing mother'. They hurry to enroll you, problem mum.

Forget your chance of early intervention; that isn't something done in Ayrshire South.
'In theory, it exists; never in practice. But flashcards should console you, problem mum.'

That wee one has co-morbid health conditions autistic people aren't supposed to get.
Despite the reams of evidence, ignore them. No observation role, you problem mum.

The special school's crammed full, so no more placements. '*We* know what's best,' they say with
    righteous zeal.
'It's mainstream school for your non-verbal children! Fight us? Then we'll troll you, problem
    mum!'

Exhausted mothers limp to the department, where social workers pen their nasty notes:
Everyone's a nail, and they're the hammer. They're desperate to control you, problem mums.

Alas, for Social Work command the budget, no way to access services alone.
Dignity and worth, tossed in the trash-can, as they assault your soul, you problem mum.

All words the parent says are slanted, twisted. Failures to record are quite the norm—
What *is* recorded obfuscates State failings. Retreat to your foxhole, you problem mums!

Can't go outside, it's better to stay home, luv. Your kid might meltdown, bolt or climb the chairs.
Don't go downtown, you don't know who'll be watching—a subtle Council mole, you problem
    mum.

So watch, as every service fails the children. The health board, education, social care.
Disabled rights and fights for family justice become the tortured goal, you problem mum.

'We have complaints procedures, our safeguarding. Just write it down and we'll investigate.'
(This evidences non-cooperation. Now we can pigeonhole you. "Problem mum.")

By then the stress of caring for the children has killed her marriage—harmed the mother's health—
A *little* pressure more, from the department, should be enough to roll you, problem mum.

Set up to fail, the woman at her wits' end. Professionals stand righteous, mean and clean —
Liùsaidh, make a ghazal and expose it, condemn them and extoll you, problem mum.

Before Resurrection

Alison Stone

Drunks drive down streets where kids play. Someone dies.
A white boy has a bad day. Someone dies.

It's not a hate crime if your victims turn
you on. Women work. Priests pray. Someone dies.

The farmhouse settles. Barn cats yowl and mate.
Hounds howl moonward. Mules bray. Someone dies.

Winter melts into spring. On Monday, no
Gun laws are passed. On Tuesday, someone dies.

What is more tragic, never-uttered love,
words stuck in throats, or the way someone dies?

Blue plus-sign on a stick. Cancer in blood.
A new baby's on the way. Someone dies.

Where race meets misogyny, a man walks
into a spa. Bullets spray. Someone dies.

Man down. The ambulance trapped. When traffic
or dumb drivers cause delay, someone dies.

Words are knives. "Grab her by the," "Kung Flu." On
our screens, in instant replay, someone dies.

You tell the oldest stories, Alison.
Someone's in charge. Someone's prey. Someone dies.

With Rilke

Eric Torgersen

"Rilke was a jerk."
— John Berryman

Some find true and lasting light with Rilke.
Others face an endless fight with Rilke.

He *was* a jerk. He wrote transcendent poems.
Why be deferential or polite with Rilke?

Let all your dormant sensitivities
soar to an unearthly height with Rilke,

but shun the throngs of hungry ghosts who seek
to make their own faint auras bright with Rilke.

Think twice before you join the school whose teachers
stoke the passions they ignite with Rilke

Some seduce with sensitivity,
others by waxing erudite with Rilke.

Strap the shit detector to your thigh
when Master bids you spend the night with Rilke.

Eric, quit complaining and get to work.
Be the one to get it right with Rilke.

Eight Ghazals

David Raphael Israel

Preface: In January of 2007 I moved from Washington, DC to Bhopal, India, in order to study Indian classical music. I lived in Asia (mostly India, also China) over a period of the next thirty months, thereafter returning to the US in July of 2009 and settling in Southern California. This selection (spanning 2006 through 2019) begins with a ghazal written while I resided in Washington, DC, anticipating the noted move, and is followed chronologically by seven others written in China, India and California.

The music that time didn't quite forget

What it means to be an American
                      will I discover   *in Bhopal?*
the music that time didn't quite forget
                      can I recover   *in Bhopal?*

on this rainy October morning my DC cab-
                      driver chats in Amharic
sargam pearled out from the Sanskritic tongue
                      may I uncover   *in Bhopal?*

it's not that I'm often depressive but a malaise
                      with autumn pulls in
I'll be to spring's dark & to winter's light
                      a cheerful lover   *in Bhopal*

the Earth is the same & yet different in
                      each quarter of the green globe
she presumably sees the selfsame stars
                      pinioned above her   *in Bhopal*

Ardeo's life wasn't an accident   but
                      can he modify the experiment?
this riddle's intractable answer might he
                      soon discover   *in Bhopal?*

sargam (Skt.): solfege syllables.

Note: When writing poetry at age twelve, I assumed 'Ardeo' as a pen-name. The name occasionally reappears as my takhallus, although more often I instead use my middle name for the ghazal signature.

[Oct. 17, 2006 / Washington, DC]

In China

This evening I stroll all around a lake *in China*
the girl with me born in the year of snake *in China*

we mention Wang Wei & the *Li Sao* over dinner
long centuries flow with antique heartbreak *in China*

the charmingest damsel I meet is a Tibetan
English lessons? thus her email I take *in China*

musicians from India! fetch we thence to China
Allah alone knows what might be at stake *in China*

so Raphael scrawls occasional verse? remind me
it's just an old habit he won't dare break *in China?*

[Oct. 24, 2007 / Beijing]

Sweet sessions of thought

Where chastened we'll keep this conversation *just between you & I*
we're facing a deep disintegration *just between you & I*
light rain falls gently these summer days long pool aflutter with wind
we're viewing no cheap imitation *just between you & I*
where challenge of work oppresses the heart one hopes to push on through
laid flat by time's steep implication *just between you & I*
what were you seeking? whither went purpose? everything drifts in flux
the seasoned will keep slack expectation *just between you & I*
sharing cigars at an ample dinner talk grows lively & loud
I've failed to read fate's dissertation *just between you & I*
people mention the Sichuan earthquake saying it reached to 9.6
things pique surprise or wreak devastation *just between you & I*
forms emerge & die souls are born & reborn the heart's each beat is measured
I'm eager to meet love's permutation *just between you & I*

at the Guanyin Temple north of Beijing pilgrims & tourists stroll
who straggle might see her   indication *just between you & I*
like a child   wouldn't you love to unravel what makes the big clock tick?
I hanker to greet such   information *just between you & I*
you resign yourself to wind & rain you surrender to time's play
all nature is Krishna's machination *just between you & I*
if you tour the globe it's not as a tourist atoms' twirl is sheer theatre
Columbus *marqueed* circumnavigation! *just between you & I*
who tumble into the weave of your story feel the tug of your yarn
that's hook line & sinker   meditation *just between you & I*
alike *trompe l'oeil* the scene seems stunning! why should sages dub it
"the poster-child of prevarication *just between you & I?"*
each day we attend sweet sessions of thought each night we drift in dream
what subtly frames the interrogation *just between you & I?*
many thoughts emerge many thoughts subside questions fade or linger
nor book nor scroll *précis* this relation *just between you & I*
now Raphael mimics a wizened gent scrawling lines in China?
he's tanked his *magnifique* reputation *just between you & I*

Note: This poem was begun sitting inside Ai Weiwei's garden sculpture beside the long pool in the "Soho" residential/commercial complex and completed at the Red Snail Temple, featuring "Guanyin with a thousand hands".

[July 5–7, 2008 / Beijing]

Siliguri en route to Nepal

Every move on the chessboard of fate *they say is predestined*
how you seek whom you love what you hate *they say is predestined*

if the world is a congeries of bubbles on what do they float?
that our boat is arriving though late *they say is predestined*

with elections   the border is closed? wash clothes at a hotel
when you cross the monastery's gate *they say is predestined*

Siliguri en route to Nepal two years coming going
when a work-visa's stamp may await *they say is predestined*

in the arbor of Shantiniketan   shade is discovered
where we wash up in poetry's state   *they say is predestined*

you return to Japan in ten days   shall we meet in Beijing?
how the sequence of moons waxes great   *they say is predestined*

room 5 at the Delhi Hotel (as it's called)   Siliguri
rather dingily charming   the rate   *they say is predestined*

there's a *stupa* in town worth a visit   time's brief abundance
turns us tourists by chance   travel's spate   *they say is predestined*

I've a clothesline but not any clothespins   hence I've an errand
what quotidian task you narrate   *they say is predestined*

not yet noon when the world grows sweltering   Bengal late April
every droplet of sweat on your pate   *they say is predestined*

when in evening the honking of horns   greets the flutter of wings
on night's beauty   how poets dilate   *they say is predestined*

Raphael's resignation runs chill   a creek in the darkness
where it reaches   while we cogitate   *they say is predestined*

Note: Offered a job in Kolkata, I awaited delayed paperwork to apply for a work visa. Meanwhile, my ten-year tourist visa required a brief exit from India (one must do so every six months). I took a train to Siliguri, a bicycle rickshaw across the Nepal border (a bridge), and a 24-hour bus to Kathmandu, where I briefly stayed at the Kopan Monastery (a Tibetan/Mahayana meditation center), soon returning south to Shantiniketan, Rabindranath Tagore's university. Later, India would refuse to grant me a work visa – hence, in the end, my repatriation.

[April 30, 2009 / Siliguri, West Bengal, India – a border town]

David Raphael Israel (with sarangi) in Bangalore, 2007

Ghazal for Phil Phillips

(May 1, 1934 – Sept. 4, 2009)

Silence surrounds me   *thinking to write for you*
language confounds me   *thinking to write for you*

all things combined   again disperse   (the *Gita*)
Maya compounds me   *thinking to write for you*

He's everywhere   within each   abode   always
parting astounds me   *thinking to write for you*

there are myriad lands   we don't recall   nor see
gravity grounds me   *thinking to write for you*

each tale returns to the teller   at last transformed
tragedy clowns me   *thinking to write for you*

on what cloud-wisp   would your silver nib inscribe
verbiage nouns me   *thinking to write for you!*

we've shared evenings too few!   it's *Yama*'s ambuscade
pulchritude pounds me   *thinking to write for you*

the game's too much & not enough   & all at once
scoreboard last-downs me   *thinking to write for you*

that I've been your friend   this   tin badge of honor
Talk-of-the-Towns me!   *thinking to write for you*

when they mention *Phillip*   *Douglas Phillips*   weep
poetry hounds me   *thinking to write for you*

Couplet 7: *Yama's ambuscade*: in ancient Indian literature, *Yama* personifies death.

Note: written after receiving news that my poet-friend up in Walnut Creek might soon pass away.

[Aug. 31, 2009 / Los Angeles, California]

Ghazal for Betty Jane

(in *raag Bhairavi*)

I have not yet found	what I sought to bring	*as a gift for you*
there is nothing now	but this song I sing	*as a gift for you*
life has fled too quick!	I forgot to offer	the simplest flower
I will dedicate	all & everything	*as a gift for you*
when the sun glides west	& the ocean shines	I remember you
teardrops strung as pearls	on a golden string	*as a gift for you*
those who meet must part	those who part will meet	it's an ancient law
flying low & high	on a cosmic swing	*as a gift for you*
Raphael discerns	such a kindly smile	at the heart of life
language delicate	he is gathering	*as a gift for you*

For my Mother, Betty Jane Israel (April 2, 1927 – October 23, 2009), in memoriam

[Oct. 30, 2009 / Los Angeles]

The poet, with his parents in Beijing, 28 July 2007

Geek Sublime

They mention   you've lately published *Geek*   *Sublime*?
so long as it isn't penned   in Greek   *sublime!*

when Kapeeshwar jumped to   Lanka in   one bound
he glimpsed in the grove   a fabled cheek   *sublime*

they've argued out   Krishna's theft of butter   so
was Mohan   a glutton?   or a sneak   *sublime?*

where feelings   in coded gestures   are   examined
her relish   is bracing   & her pique   *sublime*

the *sarangi*'s cry   derived from one's own   guts   is
regardless if carved from   tum or teak   *sublime*

in irony's circus   things turn topsy-   turvy
the beauty is gruesome   & the freak   *sublime*

in cyber-epochs   the poets morph to   sculptors
to typo is human   ah   but to tweak   *sublime*

Earth's heirs are ID'd by trait   in lieu of   surname?
Yeshu augured *blessèd*   *shall be the meek*   *sublime*

when Gautam beneath a tree   gave wordless   teachings
the *padma* he raised   showed the antique   *sublime*

does loving derive from distance   more than   nearness?
what's found is banal   but what we seek?   *sublime*

I'll grant Raphael's   no Sanskritist but   dig this!
he plainchants   the T.O.C.   of *Geek*   *Sublime*

For Vikram Chandra, author of *Geek Sublime: The Beauty of Code, the Code of Beauty* (2014)

Couplet 2: *Kapeeshwar* (Sanskrit.): Lord of Monkeys = Hanuman

In the *Rāmāyana,* Hanuman leapt from India to the island kingdom of Lankā (identified with Sri Lanka, the island country southeast of India) in one powerful bound. There, in a royal grove, he discovered the kidnapped Sita languishing under shade of a tree. He brought her greetings from her Beloved & the promise she would be rescued.

Couplet 3: *Mohan* (Hindi): fascinating / infuriating = Krishna. Devotional literature is rife with tales of Krishna, the child Avatar (said to have attained God-Realization at a very young age), playfully stealing butter from the cowgirls; in youth he was called Mohan (or Madan

Mohan).

Couplet 4: *coded gestures*: codified gestures express a range of emotions in the gesture-language (*abhinaya*) of classical dance forms such as *Kathak* and *Bharata Natyam*.

Couplet 5: *the sarangi's cry derived from one's own guts*: Raavana [Rāvaṇa, the demon king] – nemesis of Lord Raam in the *Rāmāyana* epic – is said to have been a musician. By one account, he fashioned a *sarangi* with strings wrought from his own innards. This image seems linked to the instrument's intense, plaintive tone. A *sarangi*'s body is carved from wood (generally *tum* or *teak*).

Couplet 8: *Yeshu* (Hebrew): Jesus. The couplet alludes to *Matthew* 5:5 ("Blessed are the meek, for they shall inherit the earth.").

Couplet 9: *Gautam* (Hindi): Gautama Buddha. In a Mahayana account, after enlightenment, the Buddha's first teaching was silent: conveyed simply by raising his hand holding a lotus (*padma*).

[March 24, 2014]

Logging-out

Simply to be at ease & not in pain — *seems such a blessing*
simply to be not wholly down the drain — *seems such a blessing*

requisite for accomplishment is — nuts-&-bolts survival
logging-out from concerns of loss & gain — *seems such a blessing*

multiple worlds the tragicomic soul — perforce traverses
knowing how God exists on every plane — *seems such a blessing*

from primordial dawn far destiny was smudged — upon our foreheads
feeling at length the marker's darkling stain — *seems such a blessing*

somebody zoomed to storied heights others — fell off the radar
walking the hushed prosaic earth again — *seems such a blessing*

if you should ask of that painter Raphael — where did he wander?
somewhere he's grinding plants for paint the twain — *seem such a blessing*

[April 7, 2019]

Sijo

In spring, the lake ice recedes slowly from the rocky shoreline.
Rippling blue taunts overhanging trees, glad to breathe air again.
Water whispers secrets to Sky we can never understand.

— Rose Menyon Heflin

Sauvignon Blanc

Balloons rise in my brain   granting early parole to pain
My prism tongue projects a rainbow   of sugar dreams God speaks
words I don't understand but   I'm comforted by their warm round sound

— Michael Wilson

Thirty Pieces

Loving some but not all   is merely hate for everyone we bare
selectively, gain and loss   inventing a middle ground
turning truth to silver we clutch   while we lie in Potter's Field

— Michael Wilson

Spring

Sonorous cardinals and robins   articulate rising sap
I see in the wide eyes of grass   a full commitment to green
it won't be long before   songs of lawnmowers fill the air

— Michael Wilson

Haiku

One more long winter
and the frost will have straightened
Grandmother's headstone

     — R. W. Watkins

Imperceptibly
tide fingers creep up the strand
and smother the beach

     — Danielle Woerner

No daffodils bloom
This early in the season –
Eaten by rabbits

     — Rose Menyon Heflin

The first day of spring—
decorating tree branches:
songbirds and raindrops

Purple crocuses—
only the beginning of
what longs to return

The swallows return
though the fields that were once wild
are now somewhat tame

     — Priscilla Lignori

springtime Zen retreat
the sound of the single hand?
northern flicker calls

     — Marla Carew

Hurrying along
nest repair before chicks fall –
this cattle egret

Little purple fly
do I know you from before?
friend or enemy?

— Michael Lustbader

the April moonlight
my memories of this year
hazy in its glow

— Sari Grandstaff

An early spring night
the deer feel much more at home
under the moonlight

In the spring darkness
a loud exchange by the church—
barred owls calling out

A spring storm's brewing—
a glance at the moon before
the clouds take over

After days of rain
so much life now stirs inside
the crabapple buds

— Priscilla Lignori

blueberry barrens
still blush hot pink from last fall –
spring awakening

— Danielle Woerner

Red geraniums
On sale at the hardware store
Face masks from last year.

As I leave the house
There's a ghost under the oak
In the warm spring air.

— Jim Wilson

Wind through the suburbs
      invisible schoolchildren
      swinging in backyards

— R. W. Watkins

Perched on a grass stem
a bobolink sings ... and sways
with the passing wind

Only when the wind
blows does the moth realize
how fragile he is

They may be spring clouds
but the wind still blows them off—
a glimpse of the moon

Moving side to side
the yellow tulip answers
the call of the wind

— Priscilla Lignori

stuck at traffic lights
people walking hand in hand
roadside daffodils

— Steve Denehan

I see a little
of myself in daffodils
bottle-blonde highlights

— Sari Grandstaff

next to the backhoe
daffodils and sewer line—
they have both seen worse

dandelion lawn
golden archipelago
for bee voyageurs

— Marla Carew

the drive-in movie
in our old Ford Galaxy
stars seemed brighter then

a rained-out picnic
those first umbrella kisses
in an April field

— Sari Grandstaff

Shimmering spring mist –
By the mirror of the stream
Shards of last night's dream.

— Jim Wilson

The old brook at dusk
        not even a mist now
        let alone the bridge

— R. W. Watkins

beyond the canal
pieces of fresh-fallen clouds
frolic in the fields

— Steve Denehan

horse trail gate is down
now my pricey shoes can taste
freedom, and manure

from the warming bog
that scrabbling slushy cackle:
frogs talkin' dirty

— Marla Carew

In a shallow marsh
safe from a tsunami's waves—
the wood frogs are born

— Priscilla Lignori

Spring reformation   replacing the churchyard's fence   with a plastic chain

— R. W. Watkins

spring cleaning begins
she shakes the feather duster
cobwebs catch the sun

purring orange cat
a patch of Tuesday sunlight
both of us alone

blackbird on the wire
yellow beak and yellow sun
birdsong once again

— Steve Denehan

Under the blue sky
from one branch to another
an Eastern bluebird

— Priscilla Lignori

azure springtime skies
vapour trails from metal birds
cheating gravity

— Steve Denehan

surprised by cawing
the calendar claims it's May
yeah, crows know Chronos

— David Raphael Israel

Buildings with glass walls
Caws beneath the underpass
Traffic moves slowly

— Rose Menyon Heflin

Searching through scripture
the pastor proving his point—
early plum blossoms

— Priscilla Lignori

drowning the clover
and fallen crabapple pink –
downspout waterfall

— Marla Carew

Bloomed magnolia
and one more senseless shooting—
both leave me speechless

— Priscilla Lignori

Neighbors died last year;
cut-back trumpet vines regrow—
green screens they planted

— Norma Jenckes

Hiding in treetops
and possessing the washlines,
who has seen the wind?

— R. W. Watkins

Wild turkey flushing
in a startle of wingbeats...
gifting one feather.

— Foster Hurley

this is the Tao –
yin and yang shift to balance
motion that is still

lilacs fill the air
my head becomes a bouquet
of unending spring

— Michael Wilson

covered with pollen
cars line up at the car wash
first hot day of spring

still on the front porch
shovel and bucket of sand
preview of summer

the owl has returned
this memory will last
the whole summer long

— James Lignori

The crippled fox pup
that we fed and befriended
returns an old maid

— R. W. Watkins

it doesn't matter
how empty the desert is –
my shadow's still there

— Michael Wilson

Focus on Raymond Roseliep

His Haiku Journey

An Essay by Jim Wilson

the bones of a bird
on the spring path of lovers
not saying a word

Haiku Magazine, 1969

In the 1960s, haiku in the anglosphere was getting off to a secure start. The first English-language haiku magazine, *American Haiku*, was being published. The ten issues, two per year, of *American Haiku* contained a wealth of well-written haiku in the 5-7-5 form, as well as essays on haiku theory that supported a formal approach.

In the '70s and '80s there was a shift. Official organizations such as the Haiku Society of America, founded in 1968, and associated groups and journals, rejected the approach of the '60s and earlier decades going back to the 1890s. In place of the formal, 5-7-5 approach to English-language haiku (ELH), there emerged a reinterpretation of what ELH was, what its ideals were, and how to proceed with it. This approach emphasized a short-count, free-verse and often minimalist view of haiku that rejected a syllabic approach.

For some haiku poets of the '60s who had written haiku using the syllabic approach, this caused discomfort. Some of them simply dropped out of the ELH world; poets like O. Mabson Southard come to mind.

For others, their interaction was more complex. Raymond Roseliep was one of those poets who had to negotiate the changed and changing aesthetic ideals and the often strange demands that the new, free-verse approach put on ELH poets.

Raymond Roseliep (April 11th, 1917 to December 6th, 1983) is a widely admired English-language haiku poet. He began as a poet of longer verse and received critical acclaim for his early volumes of poetry. In recognition of his achievements as a poet, Roseliep was elected to the Poetry Society of America in 1952.

Then, in 1960, Roseliep began writing haiku. Eventually haiku became the almost exclusive focus of his poetry. His haiku were published in numerous haiku journals, non-haiku journals, and non-poetry journals such as the *Thoreau Society Bulletin* and some religious magazines. Roseliep also created a significant number of limited-edition haiku chapbooks.

His style of haiku varied over time. At first, Roseliep wrote mostly in the formal style of 5-7-5:

Threnody

Nephew, go and catch
the crew-cut squirrel who has
gone the way of snow.

Delta Epsilon Sigma Bulletin, 1964

Gradually, Roseliep's style adopted most of the facets of the free-verse approach that dominated North American ELH in the '70s and '80s. This sometimes resulted in the adoption of the minimalist program so prevalent at that time in official haiku organizations, even to the point of writing single word haiku (which was a thing for a while). Here is an example of Roseliep's minimalist haiku:

goose
flight,
mine

Outch, 1980

However, Roseliep never completely abandoned the 5-7-5 approach. For example, he continued to publish formal haiku in *Haiku Journal* (the journal of the Yuki Teikei Haiku Society):

> Observing the drought
> grandfather and a lone bird –
> one with cataracts.

Haiku Journal Vol. 5, No. 1-2, 1982

I have spent a lot of time reading Roseliep's haiku because I see in Roseliep's poetic career a kind of case study of the pressures that were brought to bear to push ELH poets into a free-verse and minimalist frame. Roseliep's relationship to the free-verse and minimalist haiku movements was complicated; in some ways he followed these new trends, but in other ways he resisted them. Here are a few observations I'd like to share:

1. A brief understanding of Roseliep's background is helpful. Roseliep was born in Farley, Iowa and was destined to spend almost his entire life in that state, with brief excursions for higher education in Indiana, other Midwest locations, and Washington D.C.

He took an early interest in poetry; writing for his school paper, for example. He was raised in a Catholic family and never strayed from his Catholic heritage. He studied to become a Catholic priest, receiving ordination in 1943. These studies did not interfere with his poetry; in fact they seem to have gone hand in hand.

In 1965 Roseliep placed himself in a hospital, suffering from a nervous condition that made speaking extremely difficult and interfered with his ability to perform Mass. He was released in 1966. His Archbishop appointed Roseliep as Chaplain at Holy Family Hall in Dubuque, Iowa. Roseliep's duties there were light, leaving time for poetry and correspondence. Roseliep remained at this post until his death in 1983.

2. According to Roseliep's biographer, Donna Bauerly, who was a student of Roseliep, his writing habits were meticulous. Roseliep submitted his poetry to numerous poetry journals, as well as non-poetry journals such as the *Thoreau Society* and fraternal and religious organizations. He made a copy of all submissions and follow-up correspondence, using carbon paper. Roseliep filed all of this material in a systematic manner. This means that we have a fairly complete record of Roseliep's career as a poet, and as a haiku poet in particular. Bauerly had access to all of this material and used it extensively in her biography.

> the girl tossed a flame
> or flower in the old well
> – I'm too late to tell

Tweed, 1977

3. I think Roseliep initially took to the 5-7-5 form based on his interest in syllabic poetry, which is found in his early, successful books. It seems to me that syllabics came naturally to Roseliep, and for this reason a syllabic approach to haiku was easy for

Roseliep to access. Here is an example of his approach to syllabics:

Pastorale

The water is patterning trochees
on your musical ear, over rock
and the stiff reed and over the bleak
chenille of moss. You look toward me
with a greener hope I will ring back
the structuring word to the love I
skim, – though I can only turn away
and feel the mildest april wind strike.

Today there is no singing bloodstream
within the spring time of my body;
the sunlight is mocking a shady
pasture; and the creek is wasting foam
on banks for a lover as moody
as water that may gently grow dumb.

The Small Rain, 1963

The poem is structured on a nine-syllable line; some of the lines fall naturally into the nine count, while others are run-on lines. Roseliep will use odd-count syllabic lines in more than a few poems, including sonnets with the standard rhyme scheme but 13-syllable lines. The choice of an odd-numbered line means that Roseliep was comfortable with a structure that undermined iambics; something that could be transferred to a formal haiku structure of 5-7-5.

4. Bauerly's biography offers us many insights into the development of Roseliep's haiku. She notes that Roseliep's early haiku often were formal and traditional: "He employed the traditional 5-7-5 syllabic format, initial capitalization, and terminal punctuation. All of these haiku compositional details would soon be out of fashion, and indeed Roseliep himself soon dropped them in his own work." (Pages 96-97)

Afternoon Walk

I look back to see
the figure I lightly brushed,
now veiled in black rain.

Love Makes the Air Light, 1965

5. In reading the biography I found I needed to be critically aware of Bauerly's own views, as she evaluates Roseliep's haiku through the lens of free-verse haiku ideology, which she seems to have completely internalized. For example, when she writes "All of these haiku compositional details would soon be out of fashion," it is worth

noting that many ELH poets even today use these compositional details, and many, actually most, write in the 5-7-5 form. But it is fairly common for free-verse haiku poets like Bauerly to be unaware of this. From what I have been able to find, Bauerly has been published almost exclusively in journals like *Frogpond* and *Modern Haiku*, and has been associated with the Haiku Society of America. This is a prescription for misunderstanding what is going on with English-language haiku. There is much of value in Bauerly's biography; but for someone like myself, who takes a formal approach to haiku and writes in 5-7-5, uses initial capitals and other 'out of fashion' structures (as most ELH poets do), I find I have to be alert to missteps and misdirections.

6. Bauerly frames this shift in Roseliep's approach to haiku from a formal, 5-7-5 approach to a free-verse and sometimes minimalist approach, in a section titled 'Form: overcoming 5-7-5' (the word 'overcoming' is uncapitalized in the original). Bauerly writes, "Until the early 1970s, Roseliep hewed closely to the 5-7-5 syllable norm for haiku, but thereafter, his near-haiku and haiku were written in any line and syllable count that he fancied, usually with lines shorter than the norm. [...] Roseliep was not concerned that the content of his haiku be chopped into proper syntactical units, and he was a fan of using enjambment for poetic purposes. His daring won him both ardent admirers and caustic critics." (Pages 202, 203)

Notice how Bauerly titles this section as 'overcoming 5-7-5'. In another part of this section Bauerly refers to 5-7-5 as "rigid". This is a common trope in which free-verse haiku poets frame 5-7-5 haiku. They often refer to 5-7-5 as 'rigid' and talk about 'overcoming' the limitations of such rigidity. This way of framing the debate is called 'poisoning the well'; the inserting of an evaluation into the description. That all the great Japanese haiku poets adhered to this 'rigid' pattern does not seem to matter and is never really addressed.

7. You can think of history as a type of storytelling; it's not the same as fiction, but well-written history has many elements of good fiction. The story free-verse ELH poets tell themselves is that of leaving behind the rigid and restrictive and naive approach of 5-7-5 and entering into the more expansive, more subtle, and more free region of free-verse haiku. It is a type of hero's journey with the free-verse ELH poet being the hero.

8. Left out of these discussions is the fact that free-verse poetry does what it has done to formal haiku to any form with which it comes into contact. And what free-verse poetry does is to make any form it touches look exactly like free verse. Free-verse poets have done this to many traditional forms, such as ghazal, tanka, and sonnet. And the results are always the same: yet another poem that is indistinguishable from standard free verse.

9. You can think of a form as an 'empty vessel'. Think of an empty cup. You can pour into the cup any kind of liquid: water, wine, beer, grape juice, orange juice, green tea, black tea, herbal tea, etc. In a similar way, the 5-7-5 form is an empty vessel into which haiku poets pour their haiku, their observations, understandings, reactions, hopes, and feelings. This is freedom.

10. It's interesting to me that some people make the opposite journey of the free-verse haiku poet; moving from a free-verse approach to a formal approach, adopting 5-7-5 after writing in free verse. I'm one of those people. And I know many others. I have found that this baffles free-verse haiku poets when I tell them about it. It just doesn't fit the narrative history they have constructed and internalized.

11. From what I glean from the biography, Roseliep never interacted with any contemporary formal haiku poets. James Hackett isn't mentioned, nor is Edith Shiffert. O. Mabson Southard is also absent. On the other hand, Roseliep did contribute formal haiku to the Yuki Teikei Haiku Society's *Haiku Journal.* Bauerly has a section in her biography where she details Roseliep's correspondence with various individuals, such as Elizabeth Searle Lamb, as well as with editors and publishers. Absent from this section is any correspondence with the Tokutomis who founded the Yuki Teikei Haiku Society. I don't know if this is because there is no correspondence or because Bauerly decided not to report on it. If there was correspondence between the Tokutomis and Roseliep, it might illuminate Roseliep's thoughts about the formal parameters of traditional haiku, since that was the focus of Yuki Teikei.

12. The majority of the haiku journals in which Roseliep was published were devoted to a free-verse understanding of English-language haiku, both theoretically and editorially. Reading this, I get the overall impression of the hegemonic nature of free-verse haiku at its height. Roseliep died in 1983, so we are looking at mostly the 1970s in regards to Roseliep's haiku interests and publications. The '70s is the decade in which free-verse haiku poets in the U.S. really pushed for their agenda and developed intellectual tools that marginalized a syllabic approach. It's not that this shift to free verse

went unchallenged; but those challenges were offered by individual haiku poets such as James Hackett rather than on behalf of an institution or journal. It is clear that at that time there was no ELH journal that encouraged a syllabic approach. This didn't stop people from writing haiku in the 5-7-5 form, both well-known poets and amateurs; but it did mean that those who did write in 5-7-5 were not supported by the official haiku community.

How things have changed. It is striking that today there are numerous online haiku groups and blogs that offer haiku in 5-7-5. If Roseliep were alive today and finding his way in the world of English-language haiku, he would undoubtedly go online and find some of these sites. The development of print-on-demand technology has made it easy for people to publish their 5-7-5 haiku without having to get past editors hostile to a syllabic approach. I think Roseliep would have liked this situation. As I mentioned, Roseliep's longer poetry contains syllabically constructed poems, including syllabic sonnets. Because of this I think he would have felt at home with others who compose haiku using the 5-7-5 pattern. I think it would have been a natural fit.

13. For the most part, though, Roseliep continued to publish free-verse and minimalist haiku as he moved into the late '70s and early '80s. My conclusion is that Roseliep was following the lead of the dominant haiku societies at that time, particularly the Haiku Society of America, and journals that aligned themselves with free-verse haiku. But Roseliep did not do so uncritically. In two sections in the biography, Bauerly discusses Roseliep's resistance to some of the 'haiku don'ts' that had come to dominate free-verse haiku at that time. Bauerly writes, "In working out a system of aesthetic for his own poetry, Roseliep focused almost exclusively on Western aesthetics and poetics, casting his haiku, for example, in the mold of English, not Japanese, literary traditions." (page 206)

Later Bauerly writes, "The compositional topic that Roseliep wrestled with most often was the relationship of metaphor to haiku. As his haiku emerged out of poems written in the Western tradition, metaphor was not something he wanted to relinquish. Indeed, a large number of his haiku employed metaphor in the same way his early poems did. For this transgression of the standard notion of haiku he often came under fire from critics and reviewers." (page 207)

Notice how Bauerly refers to not using metaphor as 'the standard notion of haiku'. One of the most amazing aspects of free-verse haiku associations in the anglosphere is how they were able to conjure 'standards' that had absolutely no basis in traditional Japanese haiku or even most English-language haiku. How these associations were able to do this is a topic for another essay (and it's complicated), but it really is remarkable. Roseliep was simply too good a poet to buy into sidelining something like metaphor, and he was too confident of his poetic craft as well.

The March day is cold –
last year's debris hides the bronze
with my sister's name

Modern Haiku, Vol. 28, No. 2, 1997

14. My feeling is that formal, 5-7-5 haiku and free-verse haiku had, by the time

Roseliep engaged with them, become two distinct poetic forms. They shared common roots, but they had different purposes and strategies of expression. In this overview I have selected a number of Roseliep's formal haiku. The effect of looking at the formal haiku apart from the free-verse haiku is to see their formal relationships to each other, and to see their own integrity. For example, I hadn't thought of Roseliep as skillful with the use of end-rhyme in haiku; but it comes up with surprising frequency. I can't recall anyone pointing that out. The reason, I think, that it is overlooked, is that when the formal haiku are intermingled with the free-verse haiku (which never rhyme), it's difficult to see the distinctive features of former. I think it would be helpful to publish all of his formal haiku in their own volume, as this would bring to the foreground his approach to constructing a 5-7-5 syllabic haiku.

> Beauty, be patient,
> be, while I shelve Aquinas:
> hills, wait till I come.

Poetry Chicago, Vol. 112, No. 6, 1966

15. Roseliep, a Catholic priest living in Iowa, interacting with the emerging haiku journals and associations almost exclusively by submission and letters, is a case study in how the currents and tides of opinions on what direction English-language haiku should take impacted one poet. Roseliep was both strongly influenced by these tides, as I can see by his adoption of free-verse structure and, on occasions, minimalism to the point of anorexia; and, at the same time, strongly resistful of the trends of the '70s when they impinged on his understanding of poetry and its craft.

> campfire extinguished,
> the woman washing dishes
> in a pan of stars

Listen to the Light, 1980

Bibliography

The Collected Haiku of Raymond Roseliep, edited by Randy & Shirley Brooks; Brooks Books, Taylorville, IL., 2018
Listen to Light, Raymond Roseliep; Alembic Press, Ithaca, New York, 1980
Love Makes the Air Light, Raymond Roseliep, W. W. Norton & Company, Inc., New York, 1965
Raymond Roseliep: Man of Art Who Loves the Rose, Donna Bauerly; The Haiku Foundation, 2015
Sailing Bones, Raymond Roseliep; The Rook Press, Ruffsdale, Pennsylvania, 1978
The Small Rain, Raymond Roseliep; The Newman Press, Westminster, MD, 1963
100 Haiku for 100 Years: A Celebration of Raymond Roseliep; Brooks Books, Taylorville, Illinois, 2017

A Haiku Calendar

David Shields

January

minutes before dusk
    the frost on the fields just clears
        the forest's shadow

February

on the cold doorstep
    the postman hands me red bills,
        an azure postcard

March

somebody has turned
    the signpost to my village
        down a no-through road

April

beside the new road
    the farmer is cutting down
        the wayfaring tree

May

the forest clearing
    reveals another forest –
        of purple orchids

June

the ford a trickle
    laughing young children clamber
        on the still-locked gates

July

July in Seville
    graffiti on the whitewashed
        monastery wall

August

a hot August day
    but now the cut grass begins
        to smell of autumn

September

a Sunday postbox
    but I withhold my letters –
        a new spider web

October

now mid-October
    near the shore the blackberries
        are preserved with salt

November

cold as a stone dog
    under my numb feet, last night's
        hot water bottle

December

ice on the birdbath
    the robin alights and cocks
        a quizzical head

Haibun: We're in Never-Never Land

For Sangeeta Gundecha

David Raphael Israel

The place is called *Sham-e-Bhopal* – the Pride of Bhopal – and is what one would have to call a concept restaurant. The concept is everywhere evident in design & decor, in the attire of waiters, in graphics & nomenclature of the menu & in every musical selection of the live singers – their songs now wafting on the night air as we amble up the slope. It's pure Railroad Kitsch: *the Indian Railway Experience* as envisaged through rosy-hued lenses of a romantic recollection, encircled by green tendrils creeping up from rich, dark loam of Olden Celluloid.

This is where they're taking me for my 51st birthday? It's the first I'll celebrate in my new life as an American expat on the subcontinent. I don't need to follow the particular Urdu ghazal intoned by an old-style-*filmi* crooner to catch the basic drift. We're in Never-Never Land.

With the belovèd
we recall those bygone days
of partings meetings

cute railway stations!
O adorable train-cars!
nostalgic for when?

whom was one greeting?
whither wound one's journeying?
our life is fiction

Note: In January of 2007 I moved from Washington, DC to Bhopal, India, in order to study Indian classical music. I lived in Asia (mostly India, also China) over a period of the next thirty months, thereafter returning to the US in July of 2009 and settling in Southern California. This haibun dates from my time in Bhopal.

[May 20th, 2007 / Bhopal, Madhya Pradesh, India]

Celebrating 'Holi' in Bhopal, 2007

Life's A Cherry Blossom

"This too shall pass." – Sufi adage often attributed to Fariduddin Attar (R.A.)

Muhammad Sallahudin Bin Abdul Rahim

Like glittering stars hanging onto the petals, the morning dew silently adorns the pink canopy; its dripping sound lost amidst the noise of my hastening footsteps.

> Morning drizzle comes
> sakuras already wet
> with last night's dew drops

The blossoming cherry tree is not only a kaleidoscope of precious ephemeral moments, but also beautiful eternal memories of *her*; the only thing that the wind can't snatch from me.

> Raindrops have since ceased
> wind comes out from its hiding
> afternoon pink breeze

The silky zephyr continues to flow gently throughout the spring season, liberating the sakura petals without favour; illuminating my understanding of life as I clasp my late wife's necklace beside my heartbeat.

> Hanami's lesson
> rosy life fleets like the wind
> life's impermanence

The sakura petals fall like my teardrops as they listen to my heart pounding the poignant tune of life lost. Farewell to our season. Farewell, my beloved.

> End of hanami
> like the cherry blossom tree
> my heart is left bare

The sacred cycle of sakuras blooming and withering has been repeated for centuries without fail—bare but never barren; but when that time will come of my liberation from this grief, remains a secret.

> My heart's bare branches
> reaching out to God's promise
> of tomorrow's bloom

Senryu (or Haiku in a Lighter Vein)

Halfway through the month
and my taxes not done yet—
spring fever delays

    — Priscilla Lignori

hibernation ends
another Covid springtime
we smile behind masks

    — Steve Denehan

Afraid to check in
on old friends and relatives—
Covid-19 spring

    — James Lignori

Derelict drugstore
    the smell of hockey-card gum
    and Gold Key comics

Downloading issues
of old *Tales to Astonish*
—and an ant appears

    — R. W. Watkins

one hallway, two souls
that's alright, house centipede –
I'll go back to bed

    — Marla Carew

standing outside pubs
cigarette smoke stretching up
springtime city nights

    — Steve Denehan

alleyway urine
campus locked down for one year
this, though, has not changed

    — Marla Carew

About The Contributors...

Marla Carew studied Asian Anthropology, and then Chinese, East Asian Studies and Law at the University of Michigan. She has been studying formal haiku with Clark Strand for the last few years. A Zen practitioner for approximately a decade and a half, she works in the automotive industry.

Steve Denehan lives in Kildare, Ireland with his wife Eimear and daughter Robin. He is the author of two chapbooks and one collection with several collections forthcoming, including *Days of Falling Flesh and Rising Moons* from Golden Antelope Press, due for publication in October of 2020. Twice winner of the *Irish Times*'s New Irish Writing prize, his numerous publication credits include *Poetry Ireland Review*, *Acumen*, *Westerly* and *Into The Void*. He has been nominated for Best of the Net, Best New Poet, and has been twice nominated for The Pushcart Prize.

Sari Grandstaff is a high-school librarian. Her work has appeared in *TheNewVerse.News* and other print and online journals. In March of 2018 she had one of her haiku displayed just a few short blocks from the White House. She is a member of the Haiku Society of America and the Hudson Valley Haiku-Kai. She is also the founder of National Haiku Poetry Day, which has since come under the auspices of The Haiku Foundation. She resides in Woodstock, New York, with her husband and three children.

Rose Menyon Heflin is an emerging poet and artist from Wisconsin. So far, her work has appeared in *Argot Magazine*, *the Aurorean*, *Haiku Journal*, *Haikuniverse*, *One Sentence Poems*, and the Wisconsin Fellowship of Poets' Calendar. She also has work forthcoming in *Bramble* and *Three Line Poetry*.

Foster Hurley is a member of the Hudson Valley Haiku-kai. His emails and submissions keep going into our 'spam' box for some reason.

David Raphael Israel was born in California in 1956. He attended a small Quaker school, and wrote poetry from an early age. He studied classical Chinese at UC Berkeley, and later pursued arts journalism vis-à-vis music, writing and editing for *EAR Magazine* (NYC) in the late 1980s. Between 2007 and 2009 he lived in India and China, studying Indian music and helping open the Other Shore Arts gallery in Beijing. He has also explored oil-painting and filmmaking. His ghazals have been included in two anthologies: *Ravishing DisUnities: Real Ghazals in English* (2000) and *Here and Now: the contemporary poetry of Delhi* (2008). His poems have appeared sporadically in various journals, including *Tamarind*, *Ocho*, *Cha*, and *Voice & Verse*. Oftentimes pursuing an experimental dialogue with traditional forms, Israel has lived in the Los Angeles area since 2009.

Norma Coleman Jenckes, born and raised in Pawtucket, RI, earned her PhD (Illinois, 1974) in Dramatic Literature and taught at Bryant University, University of Cincinnati, and Union Institute and University. She founded and edited for nineteen years the journal *American Drama*, and published extensively on Bernard Shaw, Edward Albee, and Canadian theatre. A poet and playwright, Jenckes has had several plays produced and has her poems published in such journals as *Ambit, The Paris Review, Antigonish Review, Appalachian Heritage, Origami Project* and others. She also published a volume of poetry, *Dementia: That Undiscovered Country*. A Yaddo Fellow and a Fulbright Senior Scholar, she has taught and lived in Ireland, India and Romania.

James Lignori taught high-school English for 34 years, and is the recipient of the N.Y. State's English Council's Excellence in Teaching award. A life-long spiritual seeker, he has studied many traditions, and has been a student of Richard Rohr, Clark Strand and other spiritual teachers. In the last twenty years, he has facilitated many spiritual groups. He currently offers Spiritual Companioning to individuals and groups. He is an active member of Hudson Valley Haiku-kai, a group of poets that meet to share and discuss their haiku poems.

Priscilla Lignori is the winner of numerous international awards for haiku poetry, including the 2013 Basho Award and the 2016 Kiyoshi and Kiyoko Tokutomi Memorial Haiku Contest. The founder and teacher of Hudson Valley Haiku-kai, a haiku group that meets once a month, she has published one book of haiku poetry, *Beak Open, Feet Relaxed: 108 Haiku.* She is a psychotherapist in private practice in New York State.

Liùsaidh (L. J. McDowall) is a writer, activist and award-nominated poet from beyond the wall. Prior to sliding to the bottom of society, she worked in the legal profession. She lived for extended periods in Asia and Latin America, before returning to her native Scotland. Her poetry and short fiction have been published extensively online and in print, notably in *Measure,* the *World Haiku Review, Green Egg Magazine, Eastern Structures,* the *Rat's Ass Review,* and many others. Her anthology of poetry and short fiction, *Unseelie Songs: Gothic Poems and Mythic Tales*, was published in 2017, and she was executive editor of *Quarterday: A Journal of Classical Poetry* from 2015 to 2018. An anarcho-feminist, she remains a menace to a decent well-ordered society.

Michael Lustbader studied at Columbia University in NYC, as well as Adephi University in Garden City, New York. An accomplished photographer as well as a poet, he resides in Lakeway, Texas.

Muhammad Sallahudin Bin Abdul Rahim found his passion for poetry while taking the Creative Writing module in Ngee Ann Polytechnic. He was born and raised in Singapore. An introvert and minimalist by nature, he prefers solitary activities such as reading and taking nature walka in parks and beaches. He hopes to publish more poems in the future and become an established poet one day.

David Shields, originally from Kent, has lived in Wales for twenty years and is a graduate of Sheffield Hallam University's Writing MA programme. He is a member of Brecon Beacons Stanza, and has edited a selection of members' work entitled *Sestet* (Brazen Calyx Press, 2019). He has contributed poems, essays and reviews to a variety of publications, and was commended in the Frogmore Poetry Competition in 2019. He is interested in form in all its aspects, and has published two collections of light verse, with a third in preparation. He currently resides in Merthyr Vale.

Alison Stone has published six full-length collections: *Caught in the Myth* (2019), *Dazzle* (2017), *Masterplan* (a book of collaborative poems with Eric Greinke, 2018), *Ordinary Magic* (2016), *Dangerous Enough* (2014), and *They Sing at Midnight*, which won the 2003 Many Mountains Moving Poetry Award; as well as three chapbooks. Her poems have appeared in *The Paris Review*, *Poetry, Ploughshares*, *Barrow Street, Poet Lore*, and many other journals and anthologies. She has been awarded *Poetry*'s Frederick Bock Prize and the *New York Quarterly*'s Madeline Sadin Award. She was the 2017 recipient of LitSpace St. Petersburg Writer's Residency. She is also a painter and the creator of The Stone Tarot. A licensed psychotherapist, she has private practices in NYC and Nyack.

Eric Torgersen has published six books and chapbooks of poetry, two of fiction, and a full-length study of Rainer Maria Rilke and Paula Modersohn-Becker. He also translates German poetry, especially that of Rainer Maria Rilke and Nicolas Born. He was born in Huntington, New York. He holds a BA in German Literature from Cornell University; after two years in the Peace Corps in Ethiopia, he earned an MFA in poetry from the University of Iowa. He retired in the spring of 2008 after 38 years of teaching Writing at Central Michigan University. He lives in Mt. Pleasant, Michigan with his wife, the quilt artist Ann Kowaleski. He was recently made Honorary Chancellor of the Poetry Society of Michigan.

R. W. Watkins created and published *Contemporary Ghazals*, the world's first English-language journal dedicated to the ghazal form. He is the only Canadian included in Agha Shahid Ali's *Ravishing DisUnities*, the world's first anthology of English-language ghazals. In the 1990s and 2000s, Watkins's haiku and related verse appeared most prominently in *Lynx*, *RAW NerVZ Haiku* and Haiku Canada publications. He also published three chapbooks of said poetry. Online, he edits *The Comics Decoder* journal, and has served as an assistant poetry editor at *Red Fez*. His major works include *Trinity*, which collects his aforementioned chapbooks with bonus material; *Direct Lines To Hell*, a collection of his early free verse; and *The Rites of Summer*, an experimental novella set amidst the youthful decadence of Eastern Canada in 1980. *Waka-Cola: A Tanka Guide to Pop Art* and *small flowers crack concrete: eyeku and conceptual minimalism* are his latest chapbooks.

Jim Wilson has led a life that has many twists and turns. He worked on the trans-Alaska pipeline, studied in Korea and Japan, and is a former Buddhist monk and prison chaplain. He currently runs a spiritual book and tea shop in northern California. He is also a member of a local Quaker group. A dozen books of poetry to his credit, Wilson has a strong interest in syllabic forms, which is the focus of his *Shaping Words* blog. In yet another existence, Wilson was better known as Tundra Wind, the creator and publisher of *APA-Renga*—or *Lynx*, as incoming editor Terri Lee Grell renamed it—the world's first English-language journal dedicated to the Japanese linked-verse form.

Michael Wilson, a writer living in Lexington, Kentucky, has had work published in several small journals, including *Appalachian Heritage*, *Solidago*, *Frogpond*, *Cagibi*, *Stoneboat* and *The Aurorean*.

Danielle Woerner is a singer, writer and teacher who lives on the Downeast Maine coast, where she is co-founder and President of the Sunrise County Arts Institute. Her haiku have been published in the Hudson Valley arts/culture monthly *Chronogram* and the *Three Nations Anthology: Native, Canadian & New England Writers* (Resolute Bear Press, 2017). Her features and op-ed pieces have appeared in *Classical Singer*, *New Music Connoisseur*, *Hudson Valley* magazine and *Newsweek*. Her reporting for weekly newspapers was acknowledged in 2018 by the National Federation of Press Women. Woerner, also a BMI-affiliated songwriter, began writing haiku in earnest ten years ago—initially to recover from generating a 50,000-word NaNoWriMo novel manuscript in thirty days—and joined the Hudson Valley Haiku-kai in 2013.

www.ingramcontent.com/pod-product-compliance
Lightning Source LLC
Chambersburg PA
CBHW060620120726
48002CB00010B/3046